12 WOMEN IN THE SPACE INDUSTRY

by Marne Ventura

12
STORY LIBRARY
MORE TO EXPLORE

www.12StoryLibrary.com

12-Story Library is an imprint of Bookstaves.

Photographs ©: NASA, cover, 1; RIA Novosti archive, image #612748/Alexander Mokletsov/CC3.0, 4; atomtetsuwan2002/CC2.0, 4; Nick Ansell/Associated Press, 5; NASA, 6; Rena Schild/Shutterstock.com, 7; NASA, 7; Bryan Jones/CC2.0, 8; BBC/YouTube, 9; NASA, 10; NASA Johnson/CC2.0, 11; Alberto E. Rodriguez/Getty Images, 12; NASA, 13; Robert Markowitz/NASA, 14; NASA, 15; Bill Stafford and Allison Bills/NASA, 16; NASA, 17; NASA Johnson/CC2.0, 18; NASA Johnson/CC2.0, 19; NASA, 20-29

ISBN
9781632357830 (hardcover)
9781632358929 (paperback)
9781645820635 (ebook)

Library of Congress Control Number: 2019938616

Printed in the United States of America
September 2019

About the Cover
Kalpana Chawla in 2002.

Access free, up-to-date content on this topic plus a full digital version of this book. Scan the QR code on page 31 or use your school's login at 12StoryLibrary.com.

Table of Contents

1

Valentina Tereshkova: First Woman in Space

Valentina Tereshkova in 1969 (left) and in her spacesuit in 1963.

Valentina Tereshkova was a Soviet cosmonaut. She was born in 1937 in Russia. Her mother worked in a factory. Her father drove a tractor. He was killed in action during a war between the Soviet Union and Finland in 1939. Tereshkova dropped out of school when she was 16 and worked in a factory. She kept up her studies by mail.

She also learned to skydive. She made her first jump in 1959, when she was 22. She became active in politics and joined the Communist Party. Vostok was the Soviet Union's space program. The Soviet Union and the United States were competing to set records in space. In 1961, cosmonaut Yuri Gagarin became the first man in space. The United States had no women military pilots at the

Tereshkova in front of *Vostok 6*, the spacecraft she piloted into space.

time. The Soviets thought sending a woman into space would be a victory over their rival.

Tereshkova's skill at skydiving earned her a chance to try out to be a cosmonaut. She and four other women competed for the job. They were all skydivers. They trained for several months and took exams. In 1963, Tereshkova, then 25 years old, was chosen. She was launched aboard *Vostok 6* and became the first woman to fly in space. The flight lasted almost three days.

48

Number of times Valentina Tereshkova circled Earth aboard *Vostok 6*

- The spacecraft wasn't capable of landing. On the way back, Tereshkova had to eject from it and parachute down to Earth.
- For her history-making flight, she was given the title Hero of the Soviet Union.
- She later received the United Nations Gold Medal of Peace.

THINK ABOUT IT

Tereshkova never got to fly into space again. She says she still hopes to go to Mars. Would you want to fly into space? Why or why not?

2

Sally Ride: First American Woman in Space

Sally Ride in 1984.

Sally Ride was an American astronaut. Born in California in 1951, she planned to be a professional tennis player. She studied English and physics at Stanford University. She graduated in 1973. She earned her PhD from Stanford in 1978. That year, NASA picked her to be one of the first six women astronaut candidates. She was trained and tested. She got a pilot's license. She was assigned to the *Challenger* mission. In 1983, Ride became the first American woman in space.

Her first shuttle mission lasted six days. She helped launch two satellites. Ride and the other crew members did experiments. On her second *Challenger* flight in 1984, Kathryn Sullivan was also a crew member. This was the first space shuttle crew with two women. Ride was getting

SALLY RIDE AND SPORTS

Ride began playing tennis when she was 10. She won a tennis scholarship to a private school. She was ranked in the top 20 in her league. Being good at sports helped Ride get into NASA. In addition to her skills in science, she was chosen for being good at parachute jumping and water survival.

2013

Year when Sally Ride was awarded the Presidential Medal of Freedom

- President Barack Obama gave her the medal.
- Ride wrote seven children's books about space exploration.
- She started a nonprofit called Sally Ride Science to foster children's interest in STEM.

ready for a third flight when the *Challenger* exploded, killing everyone on board. This disaster caused NASA to stop shuttle flights for two years.

Ride left NASA in 1987. She became a physics professor at the University of San Diego in California. She was also director of its California Space Institute. She was head of Space.com from 1999 to 2000. This website posts information about space. Ride started programs to promote science education. She was an advocate of STEM education for girls.

Ride (right) with Kathryn Sullivan, performing experiments in space in 1984.

3

Maggie Aderin-Pocock: Space Educator

Maggie Aderin-Pocock is a British space scientist. She was born in England in 1968. Her parents were from Nigeria. They divorced when she was four. After that, she moved around to 13 different homes and schools.

As a child, Aderin-Pocock loved looking up at the stars. Her favorite TV show was about aliens on an imaginary planet. She hated school. When she was eight, she was told she had dyslexia. This is a condition that makes it difficult to learn to read and write.

Aderin-Pocock became interested in science. She began reading science books to find out more. Her reading and writing skills improved. So did her grades. Aderin-Pocock's father told her she could do anything if she tried hard enough. She began to study physics. In one class, she made a telescope. She realized she

Maggie Aderin-Pocock in 2017.

Aderin-Pocock has been the presenter of *The Sky at Night* TV program on astronomy since 2013.

250,000+
Approximate number of people who have seen Maggie Aderin-Pocock's space talks

- She says role models should be real people like herself.
- She tells her audiences that failure isn't a problem, just a step along the way.
- In 2009, Aderin-Pocock was made a Member of the Most Excellent Order of the British Empire (MBE).

loved the hands-on part of science. She would later get her PhD in mechanical engineering.

After college, Aderin-Pocock worked on a missile warning system for the British Ministry of Defense. Then she got a job in Chile. She led a team of 17 people who built a telescope in the foothills of the Andes.

Aderin-Pocock now speaks to audiences about space science. She has a TV show about astronomy, space, and the solar system. She travels around England to speak to children. Her goal is to inspire them to love space science and to follow their dreams.

4

Roberta Bondar: Canadian Astronaut

Roberta Bondar is a medical doctor and researcher. She was born in 1945 in Ontario, Canada. She earned a PhD in neurobiology from the University of Toronto in 1974. Three years later, she finished medical school. She learned to scuba dive and parachute. She worked at hospitals in Toronto, Ontario, Boston, and Seattle. She became a professor of neurology.

Roberta Bondar in 1991.

In 1983, she was one of six people chosen to be Canada's first astronauts. She began training for the Canadian Space Agency (CSA) in 1984. In 1990, she worked on a manned Spacelab module. The mission was to study weightlessness. In 1992, Bondar flew on the Space Shuttle *Discovery*. She and her crew studied how microgravity affects the human nervous system and other life forms.

Bondar left CSA in the fall of 1992 to focus on research. She has earned many awards. She was Canada's first woman astronaut and the first neurologist in space. Her research has advanced space medicine. She was made an Officer of the Order of Canada. This is the highest honor a Canadian civilian can earn. From 2003 to 2009, Bondar was the head of Trent University in Ontario.

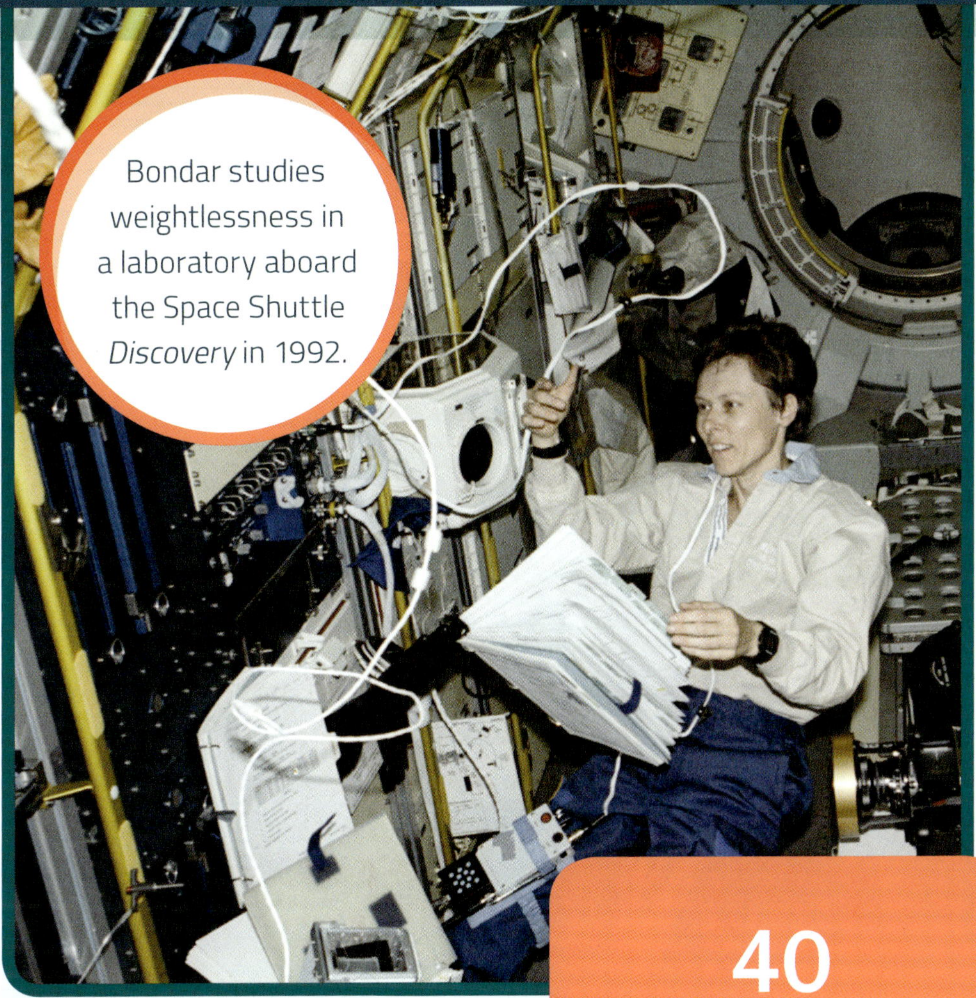

Bondar studies weightlessness in a laboratory aboard the Space Shuttle *Discovery* in 1992.

ASTRONAUT-PHOTOGRAPHER

Roberta Bondar also studied nature photography at an arts college in California. She has published four books of her own photography. Bondar has traveled to the American Southwest, the High Arctic, and the Sahara Desert to take pictures. One book includes her photos of Earth taken from space.

40

Number of experiments Roberta Bondar did in space for 14 nations

- Bondar dreamed of becoming an astronaut when she was eight years old.
- She and her team studied data from 24 space missions.
- Their research focused on how the human body recovers from space travel.

5

Eren Ozmen: Dream Chaser

Eren Ozmen, recipient of the Living Legends of Aviation Award, in 2019.

2020

Planned launch year for Dream Chaser

- If all goes well, the spacecraft will complete six missions to the ISS by 2024.
- SNC will earn $1.8 billion from the spacecraft.
- The Ozmens are billionaires.

Eren Ozmen is an American business leader. Born in Turkey in 1958 or 1959, she was encouraged by her parents to do well in school. During college, she worked full time at a bank and learned English. She met her future husband, Fatih, in 1980. They moved to America to finish college in Nevada.

Ozmen and her husband began work at Sierra Nevada Corporation, a company that made aircraft systems. At the time, it was not bringing in enough money to pay its expenses. In 1994, the Ozmens bought the company. They began to buy up other technology and aircraft companies. They grew SNC from 20 employees to 4,000. It became a major private aircraft and defense company. Today SNC makes aircraft and flight gear for the military.

SNC is working on a reusable spacecraft for NASA. Called Dream Chaser, it will take astronauts and supplies into space. In 2013, during a test flight, the craft did not work right. NASA began looking at other companies. Ozmen did not give up. She developed a better Dream Chaser. This one was chosen by NASA to carry supplies to and from the International Space Station (ISS).

THE AMERICAN DREAM

The idea that a person can come to the United States, work hard, and earn the success they hope for is called the American Dream. Eren Ozmen worked at a bank while she was in college. She sold homemade pastries. At night, she cleaned the building of the company she would later buy. She did well in school and earned a master's degree. In 2018, she was ranked No. 19 on *Forbes'* list of American's richest self-made women.

The Dream Catcher spacecraft.

6

Eileen Collins: Space Shuttle Commander

Eileen Collins is an American astronaut. She was born in 1956 in New York. As a child, she loved airplanes. She dreamed of going into space. She read books about astronauts, but none were women. She worked part-time jobs and saved her money. By age 19, she had earned enough for flying lessons.

Collins got degrees in math and economics from Syracuse University in New York in 1978. She was one of four women chosen for an Air Force pilot training program. Collins saw women astronauts parachute training at the base. She knew her goal of becoming an astronaut was possible. In 1979, she started teaching flying and math for the Air Force. She was the first female flight teacher. She kept this job for 11 years.

In 1990, Collins was chosen to be an astronaut. In 1995, she piloted the

Eileen Collins in 1998.

5,000+

Hours that Eileen Collins has logged in 30 different types of aircraft

- Collins flew on four space shuttle missions.
- She has spent over 537 hours in space.
- She retired from the Air Force in 2006.

Collins seated at the flight deck commander's station.

Space Shuttle *Discovery*. The shuttle met and docked on the Russian space station Mir. This was the first time a woman was pilot of a shuttle. Collins piloted a second flight in 1997. She docked the *Atlantis* with the Mir. They unloaded crew members and supplies. In 1999, Collins became the first woman to command a shuttle mission. She took the *Columbia* into Earth's orbit and deployed the Chandra X-Ray Observatory.

CHANDRA X-RAY OBSERVATORY

NASA has a fleet of satellites that take pictures of X-ray sources. The one that Collins's mission deployed is named after a pioneer of star science. Two other observatories, the Einstein (1978) and the Röntgensatellit (1990), came before the Chandra. The Chandra lets scientists on Earth study X-rays in space.

7

Ellen Ochoa: First Female Latinx Astronaut

Ellen Ochoa in 2000.

Ellen Ochoa is an American astronaut and inventor. She was born in California in 1958. She loved school. She played flute and thought about studying music. She was good at math, science, and volleyball. Ochoa decided to major in physics. At Stanford University, she did research in optics, the study of light. She got a patent for one of her inventions.

After Stanford, Ochoa applied to NASA to be an astronaut. At the same time, she did more optics research. She got patents for two more inventions. She earned her pilot's license. In 1990, NASA chose Ochoa to be an astronaut. She was the first female Latinx to fly in space.

Ochoa's first flight was in 1993 aboard the space shuttle *Discovery*. In 1994, she joined the *Atlantis* mission. In 1999, she was part of another *Discovery* crew. They were the first to dock on the International Space Station (ISS). In 2002, Ochoa went back to the ISS. During her four missions, she studied changes in atmosphere and space station design. Ochoa spent nearly 1,000 hours in space.

In 2007, Ochoa became deputy director of NASA's Johnson Space Center in Texas. This is mission control for NASA flights. After six years, she rose to director. During

6
Number of schools named for Ellen Ochoa

- Ochoa served as director of NASA's Johnson Space Center from 2013 to 2018.
- She earned the NASA Distinguished Service Medal, its highest award.
- She also received the Presidential Distinguished Rank Award.

THINK ABOUT IT

Ochoa had a hard time deciding on a career. She was good at and enjoyed many different things. Does more than one career interest you?

her time at the Space Center, Ochoa oversaw the *Orion* spacecraft. NASA plans to send the *Orion* farther than any other manned flight.

Ochoa plays her flute in space on *Discovery* in 1993.

8

Peggy Whitson: Space Station Commander

American astronaut Peggy Whitson has set one record after another. Born in Iowa in 1960, she earned her PhD in biochemistry in 1985. After college, Whitson did research at NASA's Johnson Space Center. She taught at the University of Texas and Rice University.

Peggy Whitson in 2016.

In 1996, Whitson became an astronaut candidate. After two years of training and testing, she was head of a team in Russia for two years. Next, she had a variety of jobs where she led NASA teams. Whitson completed three missions on board the International Space Station (ISS). She logged 377 days in space during her first two tours. This was the most for any woman at the time. On her second trip, in 2008, she was commander. On her third, from November 2016 through September 2017, she was commander for part of the mission. This made her the first woman to lead two ISS missions. Whitson also did six spacewalks. They totaled 39 hours and 46 minutes.

Between 2009 and 2012, Whitson was Chief of the Astronaut Corps. She was in charge of mission preparation, on-orbit support, and crew for the ISS. She was the first nonmilitary female to hold this job.

Whitson on a spacewalk in 2008 doing construction on the ISS.

During her career, Whitson worked on hundreds of experiments. As commander of the ISS, she oversaw changes to make the living and working space bigger. Her crew added a lab, a connecting unit, a Japanese module, and a Canadian robot.

THINK ABOUT IT

Peggy Whitson was 57 years old when she made her most recent trip to the ISS. This made her the oldest female astronaut to reach orbit. What is the importance of setting records?

665

Total days Peggy Whitson spent in space, more than any other American

- Whitson places eighth on all-time space endurance.
- She has earned many awards and medals.
- Whitson retired from NASA in June 2018.

9

Anousheh Ansari: Citizen Space Explorer

Anousheh Ansari in 2005.

$20 million

Estimated price Ansari paid to fly to the ISS

- When Ansari arrived in the United States at age 16, she did not yet speak English.
- She believes space travel should be affordable for people who want to go.
- Although she was a space tourist, she trained and worked as a crew member.

Anousheh Ansari is an American entrepreneur. Born in 1966 in Iran, she decided as a child that she wanted to travel into space. In 1984, Ansari came to the United States. She studied electronics at George Mason University. She earned a master's degree from George Washington University. At the same time, she worked full-time at a technology company. In 1993, she and her husband started their own technology company. In 2000, they sold it for $550 million.

The Ansaris wanted to promote space exploration. In 2002, they gave a multimillion-dollar gift to the X Prize Foundation. This is a group that holds contests. The goal is to promote inventions that help people. The Ansaris' donation funded a prize of $10 million. The challenge was to launch a reusable manned spacecraft twice in two weeks.

In 2006, Ansari paid a space tourism company to arrange for her to be part of a space flight. She began training in Russia. She earned a place on the flight crew of a Russian *Soyuz* spacecraft. They launched on September 18, 2006. Two days later, the *Soyuz* docked with the International Space Station (ISS). Ansari spent eight days on the station. She did studies on human physiology for the European Space Agency (ESA). An Iranian TV show interviewed her. She wrote a blog about her experience.

After returning to Earth, Ansari started another company. She is working to make a fleet of spacecraft for private use.

Ansari in the *Soyuz* spacecraft enroute to the ISS in 2006.

10

Kalpana Chawla: First Indian-Born Woman in Space

Kalpana Chawla in 2002.

Kalpana Chawla was an astronaut on the Space Shuttle *Columbia*. She was born in India in 1961. In 1982, she earned a degree in aeronautical engineering. She moved to the United States and earned a PhD from the University of Colorado in 1988.

Chawla began work as a researcher at the US National Aeronautics and Space Administration (NASA). She also did research for private companies. Her work led to breakthroughs in flight technology. In 1994, NASA chose Chawla to be an astronaut candidate. She was trained and tested. She became a crew member of the Space Shuttle *Columbia*.

The *Columbia* was a research mission. The first flight was at the end of 1997. The crew orbited Earth 252 times. They traveled 6.5 million miles (10.5

3.16

Days Kalpana Chawla spent in space

- Chawla was one of seven astronauts on the final Space Shuttle *Columbia* mission.
- Much of the data from the *Columbia* mission was sent to Earth.
- Chawla was awarded the Congressional Space Medal of Honor. She also received the NASA Space Flight Medal and the NASA Distinguished Service Medal. All were given posthumously.

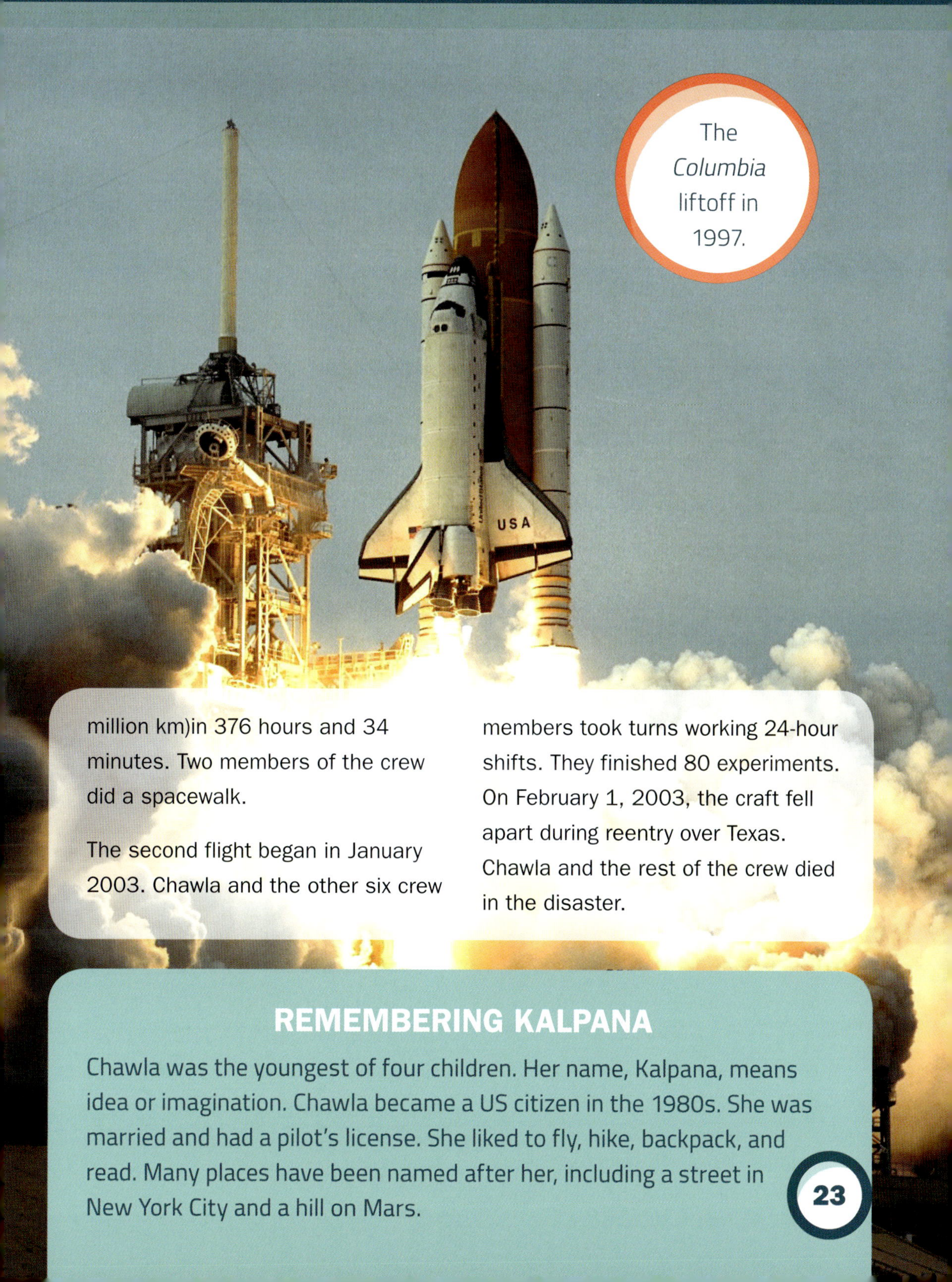

The *Columbia* liftoff in 1997.

million km)in 376 hours and 34 minutes. Two members of the crew did a spacewalk.

The second flight began in January 2003. Chawla and the other six crew members took turns working 24-hour shifts. They finished 80 experiments. On February 1, 2003, the craft fell apart during reentry over Texas. Chawla and the rest of the crew died in the disaster.

REMEMBERING KALPANA

Chawla was the youngest of four children. Her name, Kalpana, means idea or imagination. Chawla became a US citizen in the 1980s. She was married and had a pilot's license. She liked to fly, hike, backpack, and read. Many places have been named after her, including a street in New York City and a hill on Mars.

11 Kathryn Sullivan: Spacewalker

Kathryn Sullivan in 1990.

Kathryn Sullivan is an American scientist and astronaut. She was born in New Jersey in 1951. Sullivan graduated from the University of California. She got her PhD from Dalhousie University in Canada. For her research, she explored the ocean floors.

In 1978, NASA chose Sullivan to be an astronaut. She flew aboard the Space Shuttle *Challenger* in 1984. She did a 3.5-hour spacewalk. She was the first American woman to walk in space. The purpose was to test a way to refuel satellites in orbit. Astronaut Sally Ride was also on board this flight. This was the first shuttle crew with two women. By coincidence, Ride and Sullivan had been classmates in first grade.

In 1990, Sullivan flew aboard the *Discovery*. The crew deployed the Hubble Space Telescope. In 1992, she led the lab in the *Atlantis*. Her team completed 12 experiments to study Earth's atmosphere.

In 1993, Sullivan left NASA. She became head scientist at the National Oceanic and Atmospheric Administration (NOAA). Three years later, she became head of a science museum in Ohio. In 2006, she became director of math and science education at Ohio State University.

THE HUBBLE

When Kathryn Sullivan and the crew of the Space Shuttle *Discovery* deployed the Hubble Space Telescope, a new era of space exploration began. Hubble is the first major telescope to be placed in space. It has an unblocked view of the universe. From Hubble, scientists can see distant stars and galaxies. They can also observe the planets in the solar system.

532

Hours in space logged by Kathryn Sullivan

- Sullivan was inducted into the Astronaut Hall of Fame in 2004.
- President Barack Obama made her deputy head of NOAA in 2011.
- In 2013, she became acting head of NOAA.

Sullivan uses binoculars to view Earth through *Challenger's* forward cabin window in 1984.

12

Mae Jemison: Astronaut, Doctor, Educator

Mae Jemison is an American physician and astronaut. Born in Alabama in 1956, she grew up in Chicago. Her father was a maintenance worker. Her mother was a teacher. Jemison loved science. She graduated from Stanford University. Then she earned a medical degree from Cornell University in 1981.

Jemison joined the Peace Corps. She spent two and a half years in Africa. She managed health care for American volunteer workers. She did research on vaccines. When she returned home, she applied to be an astronaut with NASA. In 1986, she was accepted. She completed her training and started work at the Kennedy Space Center. She served on a joint United States–Japan space research mission.

On September 2, 1992, Jemison became the first African American woman in space. The Space Shuttle *Endeavour* carried her and six other astronauts. It orbited Earth 126 times. During the flight, Jemison worked on two bone cell research studies. This was

Mae Jemison in 1987.

Jemison working in the spacelab module in 1992.

Jemison's only flight. She logged 190 hours, 30 minutes, and 23 seconds in space.

In 1993, Jemison left NASA. She taught at Dartmouth College. She started a company that promotes science and technology education for schools. She started a science camp. She leads the 100-Year Starship project. Its mission is to make interstellar space travel possible within 100 years.

2,000

Number of people who applied for Mae Jemison's NASA astronaut position

- Jemison thought about becoming a dancer instead of a doctor.
- She appeared on an episode of *Star Trek: The Next Generation* in 1993.
- She didn't let her fear of heights stop her from space travel.

Out of the Shadows

Katherine Johnson in 1971.

Katherine Johnson

Katherine Johnson is an African American mathematician. Born in West Virginia in 1918, she worked at NASA for 35 years. Johnson did the math for the first manned spaceflight in 1961. She did calculations to send John Glenn into space. She worked on the space shuttle and Mars missions.

Eleanor Helin

Eleanor Helin was born in 1932. She became a scientist at California Institute of Technology (Caltech), where she discovered over 500 asteroids and a dozen comets. Helin was a pioneer in the search for near-Earth asteroids. These asteroids are dangerous because they can come close enough to hit Earth.

"Poppy" Northcutt at NASA in 1969.

Francis "Poppy" Northcutt

During the Apollo program, NASA's mission control room in Houston was a sea of men—and one woman. Francis "Poppy" Northcutt was born in Louisiana in 1943. After earning her degree in math, she was hired by NASA as a "computress." She worked her way up to mission control. Her calculations were key to bringing astronauts safely home. Northcutt later earned a law degree and fought for women's rights.

Susan Finley

The longest-serving woman at NASA, Susan Finley has worked as a computer programmer for more than 60 years. She has worked on many space missions. She does the math needed to explore the moon, the sun, all the planets, and other objects in our solar system.

Glossary

aeronautics
The science of flight.

candidate
One who tries out for a job.

cosmonaut
A Russian astronaut.

deploy
To place in position to work.

dock
To join to another spacecraft in space.

entrepreneur
One who starts and manages a business.

interstellar
Beyond the solar system; between the stars.

microgravity
The state of being weightless.

neurology
The study of the nervous system.

patent
A government document giving an inventor the sole right to their invention.

physiology
The study of the way a living body works.

posthumous
Taking place after a person's death.

satellite
An object that orbits a heavenly body.

Read More

Dickmann, Nancy. *Superwomen in STEM: Women Scientists in Astronomy and Space*. Milwaukee, WI: Gareth Stevens, 2018.

O'Shaughnessy, Tam. *Sally Ride: A Photobiography of America's Pioneering Woman in Space*. New York: Roaring Book Press, 2015.

Yasuda, Anita. *Astronomy: Cool Women in Space*. Girls in Science. White River Junction, VT: Nomad Press, 2015.

Index

About the Author

Marne Ventura has written over 100 books for children. A former elementary school teacher, she holds a master's degree in education from the University of California. Marne and her husband live on the central coast of California.